Massacre *of the Inr*

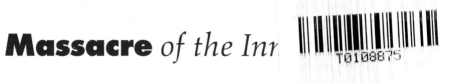

Massacre

of the Innocents

POEMS BY BIN RAMKE

Winner of the Iowa Poetry Prize

University of Iowa Press Ψ Iowa City

University of Iowa Press,

Iowa City 52242

Copyright © 1995 by Bin Ramke

All rights reserved

Printed in the United States of America

Design by Richard Hendel

Printed on acid-free paper

Library of Congress Cataloging-in-Publication Data

Ramke, Bin, 1947–

Massacre of the innocents: poems / by Bin Ramke.

p.   cm.—(Iowa poetry prize)

ISBN 0-87745-492-2 (paper)

I. Title.   II. Series.

PS3568.A446M37   1995

811'.54—dc20   94-37407

                                              CIP

01   00   99   98   97   96   95   P   5   4   3   2

No paradise unless deep within our being,

and somehow in the very heart of the self,

the self's self; and even here, in order to find it,

we must have inspected every paradise, past

and possible, have loved and hated them with

all the clumsiness of fanaticism, scrutinized

and rejected them with the competence of

disappointment itself.

—E. M. *Cioran,* History and Utopia

CONTENTS

ACKNOWLEDGMENTS

My thanks to the editors of the following publications in which these poems first appeared:

Agni Review: "Like Ulysses"
American Voice: "'The Uses of Enchantment'—Bruno Bettelheim"; "A Tree Full of Fish"
Chattahoochee Review: "The Man without a Body"
Colorado Review: "The Little Flowers"
Denver Quarterly: "Never to Heaven Go"
Lilt: "Matters of Time"
Mississippi Review: "Melting Pot"
New American Writing: "An Algebra of Innocence"
New Republic: "War Crimes"; "Further Documentation"
Ohio Review: "The New Geometry and the Little Blue Heron"; "When Culture Was Popular"
Pacific Review: "Practical Linguistics"
Paris Review: "The Future as If," under the title "An Old Philosopher"; "The Center for Atmospheric Research"; "Art. Love. Geology"; "As If the Past"
Shenandoah: "The Consolations of Grammar"
Southern Review: "Tricks"
Taos Review: Part of "He Dreams of a Cruise," under the title "The Romance of Technology"
Western Humanities Review: "Elegy as Algorithm: Seasonal Lamentation"; "Summer as a Verb, Nantucket as an Island"

I am grateful to the publisher for permission to quote from
E. M. Cioran's *History and Utopia*, translated by Richard Howard
(Seaver Books: New York, 1987).

1 Utopia

THE MAN WITHOUT A BODY

*Lacking biological resources, has he not located
himself above or below time?—E. M. Cioran*

For your small elegances, your caring for this
world, this world clings to itself its grace:
vines on the crumbling bricks.
"There was something I wanted to ask you" I said to
myself that last morning of the dream, then awoke and
shaved with scrupulous care, turning
the critical corners, gazing into the glass.

For your body, the skin of your teeth,
the hair of your eloquence, the shirt off your back,
you clung to yourself and asked me in. This world
desires itself, knows better than anything
how never to ask, never reject. I awoke and gazed
into the air the clearing cannibal-
morning drifting balloonish and doomed.

Forever. The days of Sodom and Gomorrah.
The nights of solitaire. The lavas of Pompeii spreading
into what passes. Evenings barging through an Egypt
as if history couldn't happen, as if memory might matter;
the tiny sparks of inertia already spin around centers
of Strong Forces, this physical world determines
to play itself like drama, to take the stage and make
lovers wait their turn forever, with innocence vying.

AS IF THE PAST

I am weary of repenting.—Jeremiah

Some sad Greek said the atoms swerve
and that's how anything happens. "Any-
thing" meaning not nothing. The nerve

of us to live it through, the many
and the few of us, just and unjust alike
sitting on the curb being cold; "Come in" he

told the young one leaning her bike
on her hip. We imagined perversions afoot
but lack the will to salvation—like

what you like, it's all taste, good
or bad. Then the parade turned a corner
abandoning our nice neighborhood

to devices. Someone should inform her
that the man is famous among boys,
but whose business is it? She's torn her

tight little dress, oh dear. Toys
in the window. Remnants of someone's youth
make the rest of us sick. All the joys

are out today, the sun and wind and truth,
the kind of wisdom you pick up on the street
being what passes in this kind of uncouth

colloquia. The parade's over; no beating
even in the distance of drums. No need
to linger. The day is doomed to retreat

into itself, or night. Let's eat—
before the pigeons get it. Popcorn, birdseed,
all the same allegorical need.

*

"With lots of pictures and good stories too
and Jack the jiant killers high renown" he wrote,
young John Clare, who also surely knew

streets like this and neighbors more remote
than moonmen watching us walk and hating us
for reasons too complex to chart but note

how often we pull the shades at midday thus
proving our evil intent. I was married,
faithless husband I, and she took it just

as far as she could, then turned and carried
herself inward until we were both old
and on the street the little children scurried

away from our steps passing. Oh how cold
it has become. I need more words like birds
falling at my feet, I once knew old

words like some know wines; would sniff
them into memory—white lines on mirror
sniff sniff. To train the words to lift

themselves into lyrical lines, to fear or
at least obey me—on the other hand
noble aspirations seemed to come no nearer.

What's the matter with, what is the matter
which makes, the substance of, the bland
smooth sentence I see before me shattered

by the brutal pigeon's coo? Fury and
sound, the iridescent bird makes his
two-note poem until the lady birds demand

his feathery favors. What a life his is—
nor could Shakespeare have remotely
written it better. Successful business.

*

It's all political: she hates me
and I, I can't remember what living skin
feels like. When did I last see

the fond shadow of my own thin
hand dance across the delicate tight
boundary of a human actual body when

even in accident I swerve like light
caught against the gravity of stars;
on the bus I back into corners tight

to myself because I want some warmth
and there it is before me so there
I cannot be, oh man oh woman, what harms

*

us makes us mean. Vacuum genesis—stars:
Think for a moment about the beginning, a spot
appears and from nothing anything, wars

among the particles (who cares?) let us not
to the marriage of true kinds make
impediment/love/sport of. All is fraught

with anger. So we're riding the wake
with our little surfboard self, we're balanced
on the Big Bang hurtling through quaking

time and I am crying over spilt youth. Lanced
boils and stitched split lips, semi-health
surrounds us. It'll pass. Time pranced

past us all decorated as if work stealthily
were happening but it was only luck
happening happily, full of imaginary wealth.

*

Do those things to him and he will follow
you anywhere. Such knowledge is highly
dangerous. The uneasy erotics of tall, low

stooping women, for instance, inflame him nightly
his thin sleep: he remembers the sound of the Latin
fading and the years passing—the incitements unsightly

and the furious fasting for Holy Mother Church, satin
lined and coffin-cool. To atone for suffering
children this good boy would refrain from Matins

till dawn from food and water. Around him a ring
of shadows arrayed themselves: a sun to himself
he walked in imagined holiness, for all the things

he did he thought were good. For all the good health
left to his sense of the world: on snow all shadows
are blue, but some are bluer than others. Wealth

naturally evaded such men. For all he knows
the morning still comes heavily draped
in Olympian intention, and hope falls with snow.

*

Those pigeons: they neither toil nor spin
and they are rather ugly to the untrained
eye. They live on garbage as if when

hard-edged life turned poignant and refrained
from killing small beings it was nothing
more than justice. They are wise and tame.

They know something no man can ignore
and they fill the streets with arrogance
at every inaugural parade. No more

nature than this, it is enough. Let every
creature crawl back into the slime,
give us two of each for every zoo and see

what else we can do with our time
than sit contemplating nature-navels
to remind us of all species before crime

cast out the pearls of wit and swine
aligned themselves with mud and bliss.
Take what's yours and make it mine.

*

And yet you love a fellow human
and think about her/him as if some flaw
in the brain were curable with too many

rapt minutes expended upon the virtue
and too few hours upon the vice
and beauty, beauty is a food to you

and beauty is so lovely and nice
hollowing out a nest of nerve
while you live on air and ice.

He learned to breathe in German but
no one gave him a seat on the subway. Trying
times continued on his walk through the park,
daffodils and dangerous birds. Morning
at the museums and angels buzzed
impudently above the garbage, the sweet
smell of refuse sufficient.

His Italian was better than that.
He could not account for his whereabouts
the night he disappeared. The police
don't really care: they have a
routine. He cannot leave his apartment
without peering first through the curtain
with a Dantean sense of doom.

In the future I will live in the past
he said to himself in Spanish. The smell
of politics followed him down the streets
of a major Central American capital, tall
secret policemen watched his progress,
his ambiguous back.

During his most angelic dream he awoke
in Farsi while the rugs around him flew.
Like butterflies. The room filled

with Persian carpets flapping. Agonized
women leaned down toward his face
to whisper secrets of his recent past.

Labyrinth as home. Maze as pattern
      of pauses, as place to live; and
            the necessary minotaur.
A clever man can make his stringless way through.
      In February 1858 Bernadette Soubirous
            saw in the Grotto Massabielle
a beautiful lady in a blue sash. The lady
      appeared eighteen times to the fourteen-
            year-old girl, and would say
in the local dialect:
      Que soy era Immaculada Concepriou.
            The first to be cured
by her cold water was Bouriette,
      stone mason. Bernadette died
            at age thirty-five,
a sister of the Order of Nevers.
      Other women, often Korean, some local,
            from cities in the mountains—
Leadville, Silt, Rifle, Fairplay—
      move from Denver to Houston
            to Denver, following
the lonely men who make money.
      A little money, a little time.
            Small world, grim or
cheerful. They work in bare rooms
      with narrow beds and clock
            radios to set the mood,

with bottles of oil on the window sill.
         They take credit cards. Sometimes
                    on a warm day the sound of traffic
drifts through the curtain. Windows
         high, with cracked panes.
                    Her accent thick and her teeth
bad, still she is lovely. Curled
         black hair, wide forehead
                    and long legs as if
turned on a lathe. *Maple,* a man thinks;
         Ash. She smiles
                    through him like an arrow.
When Orson Welles appeared on late
         night television he did a magic
                    trick with a Cuban cigar.
The trick failed. He was lonely
         and fat and a failure.
                    He died. The trick was mind reading,
such a pointless passion when it works.
         There are no men
                    too big for their bodies.

> B: *Up. . . . I am up. I strike with my bare heel the reality*
> *of the sensible world. . . .*
> A: *It is a kind of* coup d'état. *. . . And then? . . . You dress?*
> —Paul Valéry, *"Colloquy within a Being"*

(Dialogue between A and B)

A: Afternoon radio, its music of small deals and willing
   suspensions, makes me suspicious
   of my vision of the garden throughout that summer
   when I spent whole days at the window.

B: Rows of espaliered trees and green heavy
   in the evening trapped spots of light, black wholeness
   engulfing that edge of the world the sun's solemn
   way up lifting heavy skirts monkish.
   Sitting at a window all day was a way.

A: I saw that glistening taut triangle, her spectacular
   scapula, sun bather, garden ornament: a back view
   across pools, scaphoid skirts floating watery
   paddling herself, her reflection, across anticipation.

B: Person, personally, I wouldn't watch
   so obviously; I, eyeing them that way, disgraceful.

A: It is second nature to us to look, first nature not to.

B: See, a leaf has fallen in the water.
   It circles her memory like a little boat
   or she it, she skirts it, scaphoid.

A: She had plans.

B: She wanted you to be any kind but this,
   waking the children and pounding on the heart
   at three a.m. drunk as a doorman in *Macbeth*.

A: I answer you calm as a traffic light cautioning:
    hope is the random virtue where there's danger and dignity.
    When I was seven years old I walked from where we lived
    on the actual river to the theater where *Band of Angels*
    premiered. Baton Rouge, with algorithmic beauties.
    I walked holding the hand of my beautiful aunt
    who loved me best. My aunt and uncle sold groceries
    to the passing ships, they lived on their grocery barge
    and bananas hung from the rafters, lettuce scented the
    bedrooms.
    A conspiracy of dazzle awaited us every morning,
    those of us who awoke on the river, that angel
    of light, that band of angles
    surrounding the city.

B: So what's the difference between the tourist and
    the refugee? How good is it to be American this century
    sometimes stranger than fiction, something
    to believe in, small success, small business?

A: I have never been anywhere I have never done anything
    this is my source anyone can dream I never dream.

B: A girl hangs sheets on a line the wind wraps
    the sheets around her the girl as mummy the girl
    as Grecian drapery as architecture lingerie the body
    lying lying to the boy watching this his aunt
    hang laundry on the line on a windy day.

A: No one is as cruel as thoughtlessness
    makes him appear, nor as interesting.

B: Oh brain, you continue to fidget;
    hold still while I wash behind your ears
    gently, I was a child once myself.

A: Happily hand in hand along the shining path
    we wandered, boy and girl, Larry and Laura.
    Witches watched from their roosts, guardians,
    minding our manners, minding, mind and brain.
    Attending to duties with grandmothers, wolves,
    baskets, et cetera. As the sun set
    the architectural elements of forest highlighted
    the deeper darkness: columnar pines, domed oaks,
    fastigiate picea, with juniperus chinensus and
    the occasional cornus at eye level. But
    along the forest floor crumbs we left
    to mark a safe return failed to shine.
B: Consider the dangers: my snowy backyard
    through lace curtains when I, the last awake
    of the household, turn off the lights,
    the wide expanse of windows containing
    the brightness of snow. The children dream
    of torture, its theory and praxis, containments
    of justice. Like the light of contour maps
    shining down from the north benevolent
    as Santa Claus, cheerful lies
    guide our mountaineering. Climbing,
    the stairs then into the very beast of bed warming,
    I feel the cold air. Nothing to be done
    but the waiting.
A: I grew up on the border, you know, selling
    pictures of my sister to the tourists.
    I would take their money then tell them to follow.
    I would go faster and faster down narrower
    and narrower alleys until I could hear them

puffing and wheezing, stumbling to stay close.
Then I would turn that last corner and disappear
into some nearby bar to count my money.
Only once was I caught, and had to find
a sister to sell. Nobody's perfect.

B: As a child I slept on the couch in the living room
and the clock was loud all through the night.
Darkness to cover me and crickets to sing
but the clock grew louder through the night.
The most dangerous ghosts use the telephone.
They call on weekends when you thought
you were home alone and they remind you
you have histories and this is one.
They expect an invitation to dinner,
or they hand you the hospital bill.
Can they sleep with you in your bed? Meanwhile
the radio comforts while the snow falls.

(Thin Men)

He catalogued his hungers, and showed results:
"Whether she loves you or not, she lives with you in this
little world,
and her contempt is still more beautiful than the next world's
passion.
You were indeed a bad man, and are now merely a tired one.
So breathe
a little of the dirty air, and check the refrigerator for some
thing

left over, some little dish of leeks and dried sunflower seed to keep

you going until dinner time. 'Thy words were found,
      and I did eat them.' Jeremiah 15 : 16"

Anyone who had a mother knew better than
to love frivolous entities, the hours away.
Life is like a small mother all full of

love I guess for all the good it
does the children. Each child has one gaze
like fog piercing the city.

Doubt's instant shutters
shut against the city
in time. If

the sun was shining it was not my fault.
Half my life is over; "over"
mistaken for "lover," I looked

at the clock for assurance, and began
the climb into clothes and the future.
The twining of the climbing rose is

haphazard, significant. I watched the TV
documentary, saw the actual reaching
of a leaf for the string stretched

beside your window but the leaf not
reaching *for*, merely twisting in what
could be an agony which catches on,

continues unto death. The wild heart
turned white in the wood, as Trakl said
it would.

Sadly, there is no word for the tragedy
of coffee grown cold in the cup
its betrayal of the body, the best touch:

in those first weeks she would
in the morning drink yesterday's coffee
and go off to work. I would watch this from bed.

How sweet to align with the losers,
the righteous defeated and sing their anger
not one's own.

The small man can never reach the top shelf
(to his own shame and his mother's) but
he can be strange in his quaint clothes,

his little blue cap.
Humor a last defense he'll go
crying into the night when no one's watching.

A small fate locked him in the closet
to play tricks with his shoes
his inadequate feet.

There is no word for shame, for sadness,
oh Dear, brief glimpses of passion, perhaps
in the dark a waking to the warmth

of the living, a rhythm of breathing
or maybe I read that in a book, maybe
I wrote that in a book. But I do

recall leaning on an elbow in bed
watching her, my idle mind,
she going to work the bed soon

to be mine alone. It is not the same
as living alone, this looking forward
to the use of the bed, dominion,

a lover's absence sweeter than breakfast.
I believe in angels again, although
God is still out of the question.

1

My first date in New Orleans,
I do not remember the girl
I remember her mother, small
in the living room watching
an old movie. I felt for
the first time a despair,
the gray of television, the wait
for a daughter's safe return.

2

Knowing where to cut the joint
to remove the leg, and the angle
to slice through meat, these
elemental terrors of holidays.
The herbs fondly growing through the summer.

3

Winter when the snow conspires
to enter my house: the roof
makes little dams of ice, the trickle
of snow melting in the sunlight
stains the walls on its way
to my last good carpet. Winter
and the sound of the stain
growing underfoot.

4

Relics of summer, the Nazis
meeting on the lawn brought
folding chairs and beer and children.
Summer, and the racists march
down the littering paths
of the park: they sing
to each other of perfect weather
in the world to come.

5

In my childhood the proportion of anger
was the same as now, the small birds fell
as dead from the trees as regularly. But
the smell of the poisoned river was strong
and the curling fumes rose with impunity
while the local factory churned in the night
its own bad dream.

6

God eats at home, alone,

7

listening to the radio, staring
out His kitchen window remembering
the time before the breaking
of symmetry, the time of
vacuum genesis.

8

The shy engineer stares into his own palm
startled by the star-shaped nexus
of lines, wrinkles in the skin,
another kind of beauty.

2 History

The lovely mothers push
machines full of children
through the summer park grinding
forward. Words
glitter in the sun, the sprinklers
their rise and fall
glistering. What lovely
mothers say to babies
cannot be heard, words
without thoughts: Snapdragon
marigold alyssum and better names
than that: we must
redeem the world: a lovely dream
from which we awoke as from a coma
comme il faut like sleeping
beauty or Karen Quinlan
(deaths in life which come
to destroy the illusion
the young girl wasting into horror
connected to pumps, tubes, electric
watchers at the bedside
and the courts and appeals
and readings and counterreadings
of the texts) "A gift of delusion
wrapped itself around him—see the children
walking huddled against the winter,
walking up the path to school

their little yellow coats wrapped
cheerily against the sleet. If
he reaches out a pale hand
full of tendons and tender muscles,
it is to feel the other child's
weakest history there in the palm.
Or at the wrist the smallest pulse"
                    a gift of delusion.
As Hamlet loved Gertrude, boys love
their mothers. A sky pales in the sun
the flowers wilt seasons grow tiresome
armies of mothers turn for home as weather
arrives in sentences, paragraphs
pile on the horizon thoughts
of thunder and a rage of rain.

Egretta caerulea walks on water
and performs his daily ablutions
like a good little bird. The world
is dying, but we are used to it.
Stalking gray birds circle a simple lake,
ecstasy their duty. The sun glints
off exterior angles which add up
to any number, you will recall.
The janitor who speaks German and has
a conscience knew Hitler in his youth.
But he is clean and tidy.
Notice his bones, their color,
the way he keeps himself
in shadow as the cars pass,
their headlights sweeping arcs
and parsecs into the future.
Suppose a German became a painter
of a sentimental subject, say
herons. Mortal herons against
green sunsets to decorate the walls
of adolescents' rooms. Suppose
he knew better and hoped for absolution.
Suppose a German painted herons
because there are so few remaining
and the memories fade fast
of quaint creatures'
tiny oblate feet, broken ankles.

1

"For 'real' therefore, we must substitute
ordinary or *lingua communis*."—Coleridge.
If I find beautiful the look of plastic
sheeting and thin bags caught between wind
and wire along the slender highways of our
state it was merely my ambition to make
only wrong decisions a strange sort of humor
and a confession as in "Tell me a story"
the small girl said to me her father wanting
no story wanting sleep she wanting not to
sleep only to tremble in that particular
terror she smiled "Tell me a story" and
the father took himself so seriously
to make something up like a story not of
heroes' horror but of a little girl
sleeping as the river drifts past her
window then up into the night sky glitter-
ingly long the story of the Chinese cowherd
in love with the weaver whom the gods
separate with the Milky Way they are
such lovers such a sense of fatal humor
a white translucence shimmering in the
girl's simple terror until the daughter
fell into the long sleep from which
no one returns happy to oatmeal.

2

Against "the Luxury and Redundance of Speech"
Bishop Sprat warned the Royal Society; Tell me
no stories (the Knowledge of Nature, not Colors
of Rhetorick) but only truth clothed only
for modesty's sake: loin cloth, maybe
a thin robe tightly wrapped (if the feet
protrude it is to show how cold she is,
and dumb—W.S.) All this you will find in the
dictionary where it has been preserved
forever—since it is beautiful and
true.—William Carlos Williams.

3

Did you hear the one about the priest the
Rabbi and the Mullah taking their shaggy
dog for a walk? Realism being dead and
all. They walked. Quickly. Past
Cleopatra's Needle toward the sound of
city buses and civilized discourse, the
darkness descending faster than antici-
pated. The urban urgencies. Forced them
into. Compromise. Still, the luxury of
the Park intervened, still they trudged
along the winding path, and found
themselves in front of the famous
monument again whose bronze turtles
holding the ancient weight of powdery
Egyptian stone greened as a model of
the world. The redundancy of their

pathfinding sent them again into the on-
coming traffic, and sounds of the sur-
rounding city taunted, tantalized.

"THE USES OF ENCHANTMENT"

— BRUNO BETTELHEIM

There are alleys down which no one dubious
will ever walk again. The doomed child
among us speaks only of the cheapness

of the tricks, how integrity means
treachery in the end. Oh how he dazzles
when he says the words! He hunts and fishes

on weekends. Kills things, small and furry or
cold and scaly. There are necessary
conspiracies. Integrity rhymes with treachery.

Soon the snow which you can taste
spills over a rim of mountain to the west.
A front, a seasonal alteration. The snow

gathers in corners and glazes wheelbarrows.
The dazzle of snow under afternoon light
like nothing. The happy couple walk

home after the movie. A matinée, a treat
mid-week and full of luxury. The happy
couple walk home arm in arm in snow

to prepare for the rest of their lives.
The happy couple has been to the movies
and thinks of having children, yes.

I read by the afternoon light then hope
to sleep through the end of the century.
Constantly embarrassed by sneezes I was
allergic to everything. The lines
of sunlight through the dust of local
demolition drove me inward, a leopard
looking for some lamb to lie down with.
"Oh modern modes of loneliness" I would groan.
"Oh searing attitudes of largesse, Oh
fulsome days of good country air." Meanwhile
there is a continent whose men disembowel
themselves and any handy captive monkey
just for sport. And somewhere the various
rounds of randomness live like choirs
of angels. You know what it is to have friends
and to be unhappy in the style of the period
(Céline), to collapse into an ecstasy
of defilement, when you have the cash,
or to recall that little coin of bread
the priest would place with his own clean
hand on the pillow of your little tongue,
all clean from brushing that morning
and rinsing without taste, without a swallow.
Homemade sacraments are best,
how the balls on the pool table for years
made their complicated little rounds,

into the six little holes then back
to the green fabulous felt oh miles of travel
circumscribed, domestic and dangerous.

An emperor on a white horse on a bridge
received the adulation of the crowd, receives
the adulation of the crowd. There will be
atrocities, but for the moment he receives
the adulation of the crowd.

An emperor on a white horse on a bridge
will live to see better days, and worse,
but the crowd will not. Among these
a woman whose face will slowly melt—
history's final fadeout.

The next afternoon she dressed the children,
left a note leaning against his desk lamp
and disappeared in the station wagon loaded
with all the memorabilia of a failed marriage;
such a tiny country, such a third world.

It was the first month of Rabi, and the snow
was still general all over Japan, or so the emperor
dreamed, the emperor in his last lap of coma,
the ambassador from Kuwait outside his door,
the world wringing its little hands.

The ends of certain seasons turn false
Or fill with silliness—sexual, or, for instance,
Artistic. "I have a sense," she said, "of waltzing

Through it all, then of epic loss; having once
Begun a thing then losing track and then,
Well, I have lost it again." So her affronts

Include reading from the air those thin
And sallow lights like Latin, Greek, or some
Such way of seeming ancient, the lights when

The plane is just about to land. The dark run
Of air past the possibility of death or maiming,
The chance of land and love and later sun.

Her nights are lifelike. The lights retaining
Something like a destiny, a kind of hope or
Slight refrain, as of musical notes maintaining

Fortunate sympathy—you have an epic sense of more
Or less failure. That disturbing sense of light
Develops into a way of life, a lifting with a roar

Of engines and a peculiar smell of children—night
And the end of the runway converging, disturbing
To her technical faith in human flight.

"Betrayal" became her favorite word. Her friends
Said the earth was dying. A pear tree in the garden
Would overbear unless beaten each spring
Or too great a weight would ripen and split the trunk
In the slightest breeze. The weight of it all,
Pears and all such golden fruit. She failed
To tell the owl from the whippoorwill by sound:
Wisdom and mourning betrayed by the ear.
And curious traitors, sleeve-silk flies,
Bewitch poor fishes' Wandering eyes (John Donne).
She watched the foolish flight of birds
In high wind, watched the plastic bags
Caught on barbed wire and thought she heard
Laughter in the distance, thought that
Over some horizon there must be undulating
Wheat fields and writhing flocks of crows,
If she had never seen hyacinths, yet she loved
The word so she longed to live among hyacinths.
It is winter and the hyacinths wait.
For this betrayal of the future they will
Be cut and carried inside, carried cautiously
Full of their own fear and trembling, piled
Onto the dining table then piled into bowls
Like high romantic love to wither like some theme,
Ubi sunt in terza rima, o love in translation.
But nights in spring are full of winking trails
Of brilliance, phosphorescent fish, bursts
And battered emissaries crossing the windshield.
Bright things bringing upon themselves their ends,

Self-betrayal inevitable and invited. Surely
Hope is nothing more than habit? Surely man
Was never meant to fly, nor child to mourn.

Slide rules in belted leather cases Pickett
log-log rules sliding sexual
in the hand with lines of fine print
graven on bamboo white plastic coated
hand-made heroism in those days of
engineers into the night calculating
approximately. Neighboring numbers
blended as the eyes tired. How *words*
work is, you pay attention elsewhere
until you remember you said yes to
something that worked, it made a life.
But in the night my brother cries pillows-
full of confusion seeing visions coined
by an ancient emperor to keep awake.
Over and over while reeds grow thick
in the duckpond our work was to make
the world work with days of analog
computing, long wooden blades in our
hands while we watched the rippled
race racing across the surface during
the dark of evening at the point where
wind wiped quick breath on the mirror
held to the mouth in the movies.
We were all Americans, we boys were all
first among equals. There was a time
I knew something, a realism the conspiracy.
I wept bright coins and paid my way.

A man bigger than you and smarter walks
　　　　into his future as into a room hoping
　　　　　　　for small surprises and large comforts.
He is the future.
　　　　A sleeve pinned to his uniform
　　　　　　　flutters symbolic of senseless sorrow,
of war, retribution, and prosthetic tendencies
　　　　such as the poet's photographic blush
　　　　　　　placed artistically thus (later
they removed it and restored the tintype
　　　　to form, daguerreotype to type—
　　　　　　　to be accurate, so to speak—
blushless and sepia). *The extreme of the known*
　　　　in the presence of the extreme
　　　　　　　of the unknown. To any old
philosopher such ideas as we derive are
　　　　dreary: empty sleeves fussily
　　　　　　　fluttering.
A man bigger than you and smarter needed
　　　　to see a hand-tinted world, a world
　　　　　　　yellow and green. A man
of passion, as we say, as if there were
　　　　another kind: "How to convince
　　　　　　　you of the unknown
without resort to Art, Art being what I
　　　　like least in a timely world;
　　　　　　　I want to say it directly,

as in 'escaped alone to tell thee.' I want
to offer delay, the extreme
of the known blushing
on the sweet face of the Lady from Amherst."
The poem sometimes cried for ex-
planation, and the poem
becomes the explanation of its occasion. Which
is boring. And is *a priori* after
the fact, i.e. the poem
must be among other things
the *ding an sich*, false phrase
he overuses because *A*
it is foreign and thus one must jump hurdles to
get it, get to it, and
because *B* the idea
of The Thing Itself is the skeleton of the poem,
to him anyway, as it was to her
in Amherst. The poem
takes the place of the mountain in Amherst or
Reading, but for the poet and not
for the mountaineer: the climb
takes the place of the mountain, her effort
takes the place of dirty rock,
technical climbing
when the beautiful ropes web themselves across
the sheer cliff face, especially
the face which turns until
she finds herself climbing upside down into the
future. . . . Making one's way
makes the poem; the extreme

of the known might, for instance, be the body,
    the physical presence of the self
        within the confines of fingers
and toes which find their places in the fingerholds
    of the rock face. He had a brother
        who was a scientist.
As a boy the brother killed a cat and cleaned it
    and presented the skeleton to his school.
        More beautiful than any poem,
more clean and white, gleaming in context among
    the flasks and beakers and Bunsen
        Burners among long rows
of sinks, and sorrow had no place there, only danger.
    A man bigger than you and smarter walks
        into his future as into
a closet full of the past, full of darkness
    and simple desire, which is only to say
        the wish for something,
the sense of something missed. In the undiscovered
    closet is a shade of green more lovely
        than any tree, more full
of promise and of art than any god imagines,
    those tiny creatures too simple
        and too kind
to understand us. He knows it is the future
    because it is too narrow
        to turn around in.

1

The flamingo would turn in the wind on one leg.
And a cat. A lawn. An afternoon. The snail
had a bad reputation but climbed forever
the razor's edge to the moon leaving only
a mucous memory. This was America.
This is political. The world is rock with
a liquid center, bonbon of stone with
                    a powdery organic skin.

2

I thought of the weight of the silly planet
as last night another city burned, pity
its loss, TV the culprit. Watched men on the
moon, recalled that a man dreamed on the moon.
The angel I know best has a small face
and large hands and no power but that
of speech. He is tired but immortal.
Laplace would argue that if both position
and momentum of a particle were fully known
at a discrete moment and all forces acting
upon the particle fully known, then
the particle's motion is fully determined
                    for all future time.
Time future all. For determined fully
is motion. All interesting novels are
about a man who murders (a foreigner

after the funeral of) his mother.
The moon has a solid center. It is foreign.
It is female like a pink angel on the lawn.

3
Since revolutions go in circles we suggest
a fine delicacy, a step in a straight line,
a legacy: the maid saw things would straighten
your hair, mister; would make your sister
weep. The maid has things to do, but if
you spoke Spanish you could ask her while
the cars go fast on the interstate. The trains
don't stop for people, and trees live in pots;
you can turn them to get the best light.

History was her best subject and she voted
every chance she got. She tried to do it
right. She used to be your mother. Look
at the terrific birds, the shining feathers
made into banners for the exhibit, remember
the Aztecs could turn a million hummers
into one king's hat. Nice nature. Close
to the land, that's how to live. Put
yourself in their place, a glorious casualty
wandering home at evening the angle of sun-
light reddish and warm. The fall not yet
threatening, just a rumble in the distance
while a glamorous casualty waits at the bus stop
for her friend, a future to take home.
Here is history, how it sounds: what
                    do I love? Remind me.

4

We used to listen to the muttering
of Popeye defeating the lesser races
vegetarian Popeye armed with unrequited
love for a slender woman. I like secret
agents of my own animation, me
about to be invented lying awake
imagining that the dawn waits patienter
than lovers. I have always known the world
is full of hunger and anger and despair
a form of which is loneliness:
some is my fault, some my reward. Small
wonder there is a city named La Paz
where my beautiful step-daughter
attracted the old man's attention,
the old man who spit on his hand
then with the other hand touched
her hair; who knew? Bolivia
exports tin and bauxite and keeps
the beautiful names (Sugar and Peace
in a manner of speaking) for capitals.
Wicked step-parents learn to live
in penumbrae of beautiful daughters,
serpents in the gardens. So lie
in bed and rehearse, reverse
the regulation of the arable, all
the patterns spinning like an old
man of La Paz returning in dream
spitting on that hand as if to
                    grip the plow.

(Or maybe you preferred Krazy Kat and
the accurate artillery of love, mouse-
thrown bricks crashing. Isn't it just
like opera, couldn't you just die
waiting and waiting for Spiderman
to pendulum past the window telling
good jokes and killing bad men. Couldn't
             you live that way?)

5
Comic books, Japan, anything, stars
to talk about, loneliness works this way:
the empty seat next to you on the bus
as audience, the city passing quickly
and the weather never alters. Text
             and illustration:

Wonder Woman flew an invisible airplane
dotted lines emblem of its shape memory
a poem of the mind's eye seeing.
With a golden rope she evoked
involuntary truth from trussed
enemies. A golden age. Trust

Japanese men in small suits riding
trains at hundreds of miles per hour
gathering cleanly to talk business and love.

Here is the hard one: openness, like the sound
when you press your ears closed not like

an ocean at all. The roar of blood, home
again where the house echoes. Something
breaks two blocks away and the glistering
sound stays forever, its own memory.

It would be good to teach a child the names
of each: Beehive, M44, Praesepe, any chart
would do: the Chinese made the Milky Way
a barrier between lovers, self control not
their virtue, the lovers. If a star
falls, is there a sound.

6
"Dear ———, I walk around
these mountains, monstrous things full
of rock, basalt bands ribboning them.
The birds are black billed magpies
each with a history and insect digesting.
The wind rising whirls itself
around corners of this protruding world.
I walk around these mountains full
of horizons slipped onto their ragged
edges, the end of landscape becoming
a picture like a pretty melody, a girl.
The birds are black with long tails
and streaks of white. Like ghosts
they fly like angels. Against
the wind the birds are beaten
back as memory fills them with despair.
Sincerely, ———."

7

Dreaming on the moon a man dreamed on
the moon he said: "I dreamed I found footprints
not ours over a hill . . ." when in his little mobile
home his flying turtle-shell his pup tent
his boy scout house he slept;

a child could not nurse there no mother's
child could nurse in that moon night that light
you need the weight of atmosphere the air of earth
conspires to spill a little milk into the mouths
of babies. Lover please forgive my life, come

back and try again to talk to me. The light
is so sweet and the birds sing and everything.
We have air and summer night and insects
hover uncrushed in its weight their short lives.

3 Paradise

ART. LOVE. GEOLOGY

Ist es schön, in der Sonne zu gehn.—*Trakl*

Here is a little book of instructions. It says care
must be taken. For instance, a form of health as a
version of vanity (as when a poor stonecutter set up
shop to live off the vanity of travelers, pioneers
who stopped to scratch names and dates in inviting surfaces
but granite is hard on the amateur so a graffitist,

*

an American artist, against the rapacious
rock body of the earth did cover the good body with
American names, this national poetry which must be
written carelessly before the one war, after the other.
The view was magnificent, and the air smelled of future)
        vanity in this world, my Dear, your hair the color,
this kind of poetry, this world tells itself stories,
O famous your green shoes your fabulous wishes your
hair the color of tea and your green shoes aren't you something.
It says here you must listen to your own history, it says
you must take care, and it says here you must pronounce
your name, your own name here ——————.

*

This man did believe in the monochrome
possibilities, the way the camera once would focus
such a narrow range of color thus the *sharpness*

of the old photographs, the clarity of vision
of the American West before the development
of panchromatic films. And the movies, the cow-
boys and Indians blazing black and white.

*

"At the edge of the forest/Stillness encounters
a dark deer"—the way she said it, my friend
said it of Trakl, his poem. *Geistliche Dämmerung*
and it is snowing now and cold. When I knew her
we were young and the age of the earth indeterminate.
Forests had edges. Deer were a species of Indian.

*

Here is the world come to comfort me. Here
is a child come to follow me home.

*

The traveling salesman said to the farmer's daughter:
we are in this world together and there is no place
to sleep, so let's join hands and sing of the glory
and honor of the forest and its deer which watch us;
see their eyes reflect the light, see them wait for us.

*

Und rings erglänzten Hügel und Wald.

*

And surrounding us, you and I, love,
something like the night—at least it is dark,
at least it is silent. It seems to move
only when we do not look at it. It seems
to be the world, but who knows, and we,
do we really care more for each other
than for the world, can the songs be right?

*

Surrounding shimmering in ultraviolet
the darkness to eyes not our own, but we
have gauges to measure this shimmer.
The insects see in light not ours
the insects see flowers in violet so deep
its darkness shimmers in the corner of
my eye as if I made it up.

*

If hills emerge too slowly to see, still, evidence
remains—it's what geology says, that this earth
moves beneath each lover, slow and impossible
but there you have it, the hills rise around us
when we are not looking and one day an alp
taps you on the shoulder as you kiss
and your mind wasn't on the time; it is late.

*

This is the forest, here, we live here. Arboreal
safety. Who cares for evolution. Here, let me
love you then we'll fall from the trees like
fruit, the sound it makes, the forest surrounds
our racial despair. Oh how we hate to be human.

History meant nothing to me, born nowhere
at no time. History was my mother's,
geology Father's concern. Mine
was homework, flat portions of a past.
History meant the dead remain there,
alone and little used, decorous
or decorative. Sweet
are the uses of wealth: health
and libraries, collections of arts and
wings of hospitals which soar
over gardens where the few minutes
of rain cause long lakes to form, trout
to appear full and legal with spots.
Salvation is a smaller matter, as if soon
the little flowers of childhood, the buds
on the wallpaper, perhaps, or the trees
outside your window would bloom finally;
as if it were a little yellow capsule
bouncing happily down the highway.

There are many theories, and these are mine:
the nation is not so sleazy a circus
as it looks. The end will be painful.
I used to see Mr. Calley every day, no longer
Lieutenant, selling jewelry, arranging bridal
registries. A normal face. Hands
of a salesman accustomed to thin triggers

of sales tax, of accidental leverage.
It is good to lose sometimes, some wars;
my friend had a hero for a father
whose medals tinkled like iced tea at dinner.
It was ice that tinkled, but I thought:
that must be the sound of heroes.
Summer is more difficult than before, now
that the world is smaller, less kind.
The war is over, true, but since all sides
lost, since the jungle itself cried Hold,
enough! the summers are hard on us, yellow
school buses no longer linger at the door.

(The black letter of Grandfather's pre-war
German text—the formal face it wore,
the danger sudden as war won: an education
close-grained and echoing like heels
clicking on terrazzo. Those letters heavy
and full of history. The dust of afternoon
on the edge of the pages, delicate
and carefully planned. How foreign it was.)

"Who are you to tell us how to live, or why,
et cetera?" No Man, of course, and not so tall
as is the current fashion, nor smart enough
in the acceptable modern way, to enthrall

the crowd with stories of my life among
the savages where I was home and growing
baffled day by day, raging through the night
as if it were new music I made, groaning.

It came to me today at lunch, the sound
of women in the next booth, a voice like
Aunt Odile's—whom I never knew well
nor did I like her, but not her spite

but her voice like home-grown fame, a touch
gravelly, a considerable groan itself, it seemed.
They spoke outmoded French around me, never
to me, except to taunt, I thought. She leaned

above me, on those visits, speaking to Mother
in their private French, laughing. A boy
surrounded by the sound of foreign tongues
knowing what wasn't meant for him: toy

temptations, suggestive coils of syllables.
I learned Latin, for Mass, and did love

its terrific laddered randomness:
The Blessed hovering Virgin above

every station of a boy's new path, hormonal
disharmonies, her praises sung into hundreds
the first Tuesday of every month; and yet
Latin could not expose such shreds

of glittering flesh as I found in French,
not like the living tongue whose tip twined
into an Uncle's mustache as he leered
at the wrong Aunt and winked and a fine

distance crystallized loud there, then
gone. Crashing like German. Father's family
spoke clear English among the bayous, boys
and girls of immigrants accentless happily

German through two wars, not counting
Civil. I had the tongue for arithmetic
and spoke it beautifully. I loved to count:
precision's a tempting career, clicking

into a future like an abacus ignoring
all those accents around.
I never learned the luck of any
but English, bland and bound.

But only yesterday I heard a word
the mechanic said in Czech

to his cousin—*shop rag*—clearly centered
in a welter of incomprehension, the wreck

of my car at their wretched mercies: shop
rag. And he wiped his hands and cried
for me, shrugging like a cousin would.
I wrote a check. I drove home, or tried.

So does it count? Am I a man of passion or
child of comprehension? "Father of little lusts
driving myself home who thinks: Buy some
sentiment, a little like love and she must

speak French this time. She longs
for you, you know; it isn't just the money.
America loves you for yourself alone"
and so I go for professional help, honey-

blond hair and a disposition like
a happy banker, whose French for *dear*
sounds like *dog*; the cost of living
is going up, loving her here.

The appearance of weight, the momentum of pink
profoundly draping the tree outside the window,
this impression of the season: the bowing
anxiety of xylem, and the unseasonable rain

threatens further wreckage. Nature
pink in gum and paw. Crab apple and quince.
A man in an office wishes the world well, takes
his leave nevertheless of light and the lyric.

The Office is a concept new in the history
of civilization; a place of plenitude, a kind
of club. To arrange his implements on his desk.
He consults. How lovely the hours. How long.

But you still don't understand the pinkness
of this tree; the fullness of bloom and pitch
under this slight rain—it snowed a day ago,
and this is now May, official and finicky.

The tree is like: brain coral—any internal
organ. Silk in her top left drawer.
A loss of innocence, not to say guilt.
The not yet serious sun. A man's real work.

Suppose there were only two tenses in English,
Or four—would there have been no war, or more
Between us? Or would the scientist
Have something else to say in those intimate
Moments when the flesh turns too too solid,
Sullied intentions glittering on the horizon?
Would clocks have not been invented,
Calendars have caused no crises, robins have clung
Less tangibly to their spring perches, less full
Of themselves under the boy's gaze from his bedroom,
His illness keeping him one more day home
From school, the world less sure of itself for this?
I used to watch bullfights from Mexico on Sundays;
The bull's life reduced to a series of doors, the last
Of which he was dragged through in chains. The blood
In black and white was not so bad, the picture
Fuzzy on the GE set. I liked banderillas
Best, the reduction of man's life and animal's pain
To a closing arc and a tangent. When I was a child
I saw as a child the butchery of our cow,
Named but past freshening. The delicate butchers
Sharpened their knives every three minutes,
The delicate butchers wearing rubber aprons,
Rubber boots. The transition from life to meat
In front of me in color. There is an unnamed tense
Which you can see, like a puff of breath as you reach
In for another TV dinner, living the life of leisure.

Pei designed the building with views,
smooth masonry, and the mountains aligned
for a photo opportunity; inside are files
sufficient for forever, for fine tuning weather.

Great Spangled Fritillary, the watcher vaguely recalls
from Teach Yourself Lepidoptery, a book.
He wanted to live in a land of appropriate weather
with views of mountains and with music constant.

He wants to tell a story but no one would listen,
like opera: Black women clean the floors
and shine the walls like silver nightly.
Computers whir Platonic as nuns. Nothing

escapes naming; storms arranged in teacups
like anyone's collection, like rows of butterflies
pinned and satisfactory: this is the new landscape.
Or there is a lewd father among the shrubbery

watching daughters in weather; he breathes heavily
and the wet wisdom begins, the storm gathering
to spill across the ridge, longed for.
Daughters must be warned against sincerity

of frantic violins: "He was a man of sympathetic
tendencies," read the official report. "He was
smaller than he looked and tended to lick chocolate
from his fingers in a lascivious manner."

He tried his wife's patience, it is true,
and lived alone through the marriage, kept
his own counsel. With such petty symbols as
weather, he kept his own counsel.

A butterfly like weather; the climate like
laughter, the movement of small air. Clouds, too,
have names. Clouds leave home to find themselves.
Good money after bad, the fathers say, and close

the door called Nature against their coming back.
The funny little ways children have of making
the world the color they always wanted. Sunset.
Birds. The mathematics of memory begin

to swirl like cookie dough, like chocolate with egg
and sugar and vanilla and butter. A bowl to lick,
dangerous with delight, as ultraviolet. Home again!
begs the mother and soon the sorry child walks

that long allée as rain begins to pour. Past
such petty symbols the boy returns through architecture,
a silly gauntlet: the butterfly, the mother, the fit
signatures of loveliness. His parents at the door,

the little cottage in the woods, Hansel home again
at last, the shining path. A little like a dream.
Ours is not a simple age, and things are what they seem
happily ever after in the malicious tiny rain.

Listen to languishments murmur through the night
as one minor landscape drifts past per hour;
attention turns to allegory: given time and
consideration, you might have been a saint

born a century before. How long
will we believe anything is possible
by the ocean, if we only pay it enough.
Attention. The density of this air

will hold the wake of birds for hours,
long ribbons over marshes, flights and families
of birds attending to business. The light
descends to this ground stepping slowly

from the sun, that dreary matte disk.
You must remember to breathe, as if opening
gills: a man could drown walking home
from such a beach. So there is an ocean

still gray and full of sailors' bones
and bungled design—naval architecture. Entire
nations underfoot that were once us, ground
into sand. You could be a saint if you want

on this beach before the crowds gather, one
with it all. With part of it. One with some.
Only the rich live here, and few are unhappy.
You might as well be a saint.

I said I could face anything but facts, politically
speaking. So he handed over his little friend
telling me her story, a life full of surprises,
saying everything twice as if to prove how rare.

(This world speaking back to you is
on a roll, is really with it this time,
got you coming and going. This world full of itself
has lotteries and marriage counselors, laws

and contraband wristwatches cheap in the streets.
The story of its life is long and quaint. There
you have it.) So after we were introduced it occurred
to me I needed a subject, something striking,

a way to make an impression. I reminded her how
the set of probabilities characterizing all
possible transitions of an atom constitute
a square array of numbers that satisfy

the algebra of matrices. But I forgot, as
she pointed out to me, politely but firmly,
that matrices do not in general "commute,"
as noted by Heisenberg as early as 1925.

The next night I tried distinguishing
between the theological concept of law

as prescriptive morality and law as mere
description of predictable behavior;

she answered that constitutive, dispositional,
developmental, quasiteleological, abstract
and idealized properties, processes, and
relations and observed patterns through

experimentally established invariances
was the only law she could ever truly love.
And besides, she had noticed my beautiful limp,
a touching invariance full of nuance.

HE DREAMS OF A CRUISE

After Auden

1

Between the nacreous surface of skull
concave and clever and the soft gray
of brain (the lining of bone on
brittle bone)—an alcohol flame; flambéed
bananas in rum at his table, the smell
of sterno in the air, the waiter's soft
hiss of approval removing the menu:
It was improvised innocence, something
picked up along the way. The island
disappeared when he looked, like plot
from a novel. Watching television
with the sound off, a film in black and white
every surface in sight plastered with *Danger*:
a man lives in whichever world finds him
out. Danger plastered on every surface,
women and children first he dreams
as ships cross half-way that horizon
he dreams of roaming—*anger*
being an anagram for *range*, and *danger*
the past tense. Saints defined by their bodies,
martyrs, masochists, and gourmets.
Even God could save us only in a body.

2

People fall out of windows and airplanes
and balloons—people fall from the sky.
People will die if they fall
but people will fall from the sky.
The people fall from the sky like snow
in August. They are quiet and rather
ashamed, the people falling
like snow in August. There is heat
and the soft falling from the sky.
It is a form of opera, someone falling
and tipping his hat. The cat watches
as if amused. There is nothing to hear.
The romance of technology kills.

IN LAYMAN'S TERMS

X is X. X is also Y. X
is always Z. Mathematicians
try to keep this a secret.

Geometry is how we measure
the world. If your mother
helped you with homework

she knows this in spite of
her protests as she sinks
into oblivion: "No one *told* me!"

They told her in school answers
don't matter in themselves
just learn the principles.

Here is a family full of error
dining happily one Sunday
of an indifferent year in

a province of the far-flung
empire. The tiniest Tim raises
his glass to honor Mom;

sister drools triumphant
in her corner. The universe
smiles indulgently, immeasurably.

Still, when they add it up
someone is missing—there must be
war, someone must be dead—

grief spills the soup; crackers
crumble exultantly floorward
as if anyone expected happiness,

as if anyone had ever thought X
could be anything but Y which
is why philosophy started.

Talk to me, Mom said to Dad
at night when all surviving children
were thought to be fast asleep.

A TREE FULL OF FISH

(Nine Dreams of a Girl)

Sleep is a place where you can dive as if into water but not
drown. She knew that. It was where she felt safe.
Sometimes she thought she was followed but
she was good at losing them,
at hiding behind corners until the feeling passed.

Her mother would read to her at night
to make her dream. The parent reads what the parent wants
the girl to dream. So she would listen for a time
but soon would recall her own dreams,
then would pretend she was asleep as a way to begin
and then her mother would give up and to herself
finish reading the story silently in the dark as
large-mouth bass prowled the silt-darkened rivers
outside her windows. The flame-stitched pillows
on the couch coolly burn. She would jump
from an imagined rock and the splash
would follow her down and the bubbles would glide
with her to the bottom where the light shone
dimly, where she heard Christmas carols in the distance.
Dangerous mothers spent days shopping for patterns,
turning the large stiff pages of catalogues, turning
slow faces to the metal cabinets aligned endlessly;
Mothers would slide open the heavy drawers to find
the right red fish for Halloween or a sad little elf
for Christmas. This was the first dream.

ANOTHER DREAM WAS DURING

the time of the world's tallest mountain, the light coming down
from the North as drawn in all the relief maps, the imaginary
North the imaginary light as a clean moment. She climbed steadily
without pause and heard vaguely from below the sound of her
mother's lost voice on and on telling her some story about some
child who wandered the woods alone until wolves or grandmothers
ate her. It would be odd to live inside an animal or a grandmother
or a whale, like a bubble, the clean mountain with the light coming
straight from the North is better

it is better not to drown than to marry.

THE THIRD DREAM RECURRENT

as fever diminished the world in the eyes of the child,
the torment delivered whole and clean to her tiny pathos.
Listen, she said to herself, you are a child,
this all-night arrogance is beyond you; play a little,
give yourself some credit. She was so small
and full of the larger virtues, like a saint
ready for martyrdom as any pear ripened.

Christmas like a wave on a pond the pebble thrown infinitely
the little waves wash at the toes of all the children sleeping
around the world awaiting some silent visitation, some creature
coming to punish or to praise;

the holidays are full of this kind of wisdom
like Jerusalem, so full of fate

and long anger. To be a child who dreams is to walk in danger.
She will wake now, she is so tired.

WAR IS THIS DREAM TO A CHILD

whose father was there, whose father in the night fights the
television enemy, whose father remembers and sleeps two rooms
down the hall and sleeps with a light burning, never never in total
dark horror.

What child can live like this, with a father who was there and,
proud of his wounds, wounds all children in the neighborhood
and sleeps only with a light.

Slowly as the horses of the night she rode them down the hall
to her father's door, the light under the door, the sound of her
father's sleeping soft as something gigantic back there sleeping
sleeping:

go to him, someone said nearby, he needs you. So in her little
red costume the only daughter dances down the hall to listen to
the story of the war and the French farmhouse where the farmer's
daughter had a clean bed and no past and no future like any every
child.

THE FIFTH CHRISTMAS DREAM

of such a child was simple who said her little prayers
Now I lay me down to sleep now I play the clown
too deep now my day will drown in sleep allow

the play to ground to creep living this way
the dangerous sisterhood of dream was full of divorce

diving straight arrowish into the center of the target of ripples
already there she became particle and wave in a complex of inter-
ference patterns zebra-like on the wall as the story her miniature
mother read to her sharpened to a point and the laughter turned
rhetorical burst:

she dreamed that kind of world this time, yes.

THE STILL, STILL LIFE

The map she learned to follow was the back of her hand, the
islands of melanin, the throbbing veins draining to the wrist, the
months and years yielding:

there are those moments when she cannot speak to the world.
The dream continues into all those eels, els and twists,
letters. Nothing moves or nothing is ever still, either.
Lemons on a plate, light—you've seen the same yourself, it's
your life still

still her life after childhood stood there as in a closet or under
the bed. Anyone can have ambitions: the ambition to wake up, to
turn that corner uncaught, to leave the forest, etc. But it is never
enough since you have to sleep sometime, no matter how success-
ful your life otherwise. Think of Edison inventing the lightbulb
then climbing onto the lab table for five minutes of sleep. The tree
twinkled behind the teacher as the teacher taught that story, as the

tale of hard work and practicality unfolded under the haunted look of the angel atop the indoor tree, the tree dying the lightbulbs winking like an old man's leer in the parking lot (Christmas ornaments, glass bubbles fragile).

THE DREAM OF THE INCONSOLABLE DESERT

Sunday school and parochial discipline gave us stories of water from stones and stone-shaped bread and yet no sense of desert as tangible came into those upper rooms where the ecclesiastical present presided over the historical past. The desert still holds this attraction: as a place for the expiation of ancient guilt, fossil guilt, there are no wells in the distance, no academic camel drivers.

> At recess a game of soap bubbles. See the child
> blowing her own soul through the eye of a needle—
> it extrudes into the other side gleaming, sound,
> a perfection in three dimensions which attracts rainbows
> but contains nothing more than the used, moist breath
> of the child, the depleted oxygen and the indifferent nitrogen
> rejected by her tiny lungs.

"Writing is the childhood of the void, an exorcism of letters, of words"—Edmond Jabès

> Imagine the child diving into her own reflection—say
> an extraordinarily smooth surface, say a lake of mercury
> and the faces meet then disappear into each other,
> dissolve, then the body parts collide, collapse
> into themselves, their opposites—left hand

into right neither knowing for lack of leisure
what the other becomes;
say this smooth perfection continues, a snake
descending a limb, a lizard's tail following itself
into a crack in a rock—until the soft disappearance
of the tiny half-moon of the tip of the big toe into
light.

Among the little landmarks of a life, the hills
of desire see themselves mountains.

This is her dream gently waving like a flag across
every surface.

DREAMS

analysis of. *See* dream interpretation,   anxiety type,
of children,   "day's residues" in,   (Anna) Freud's,
Freud's lectures on,   Freud's papers on,   (William)
James on, Jung *vs.* Freud on,   Pötzl on,   prophetic,
recurrent,   and telepathy,   theories of, before Freud,
traumatic,   as wish fulfillment,   dreams, Freud's:
botanical monograph,   cocaine in,   Count Thun,
erotic,   interpreted; in *Interpretation of Dreams*, by
Jung,   of Irma's injection. *See* Irma's Injection dream,
about "Jewish question" (1898),   about his mother,
"*Non vixit*,"   at Padua beer garden,   his reluctance to
complete interpretation of,   in his self-analysis,   in
World War I,—index to *Freud*, Peter Gay

The boys in the back of the room planning to be geniuses examine the fascinating backs of their own hands.

A THREE-QUARTERS LIFE-

sized Santa glows across her front lawn shining sanctity and generosity into her bed across her sleeping face welling tears in the year's eye. Seasonal greetings multicolored stream through the mail. The visionary daughter of the household dreams triumphant. All the questions of childhood tremble in the face of bedtime reading then recoil against the necessary darkness of her closet in spite of pink cashmere and the tiniest china dogs ranged in rows formidable as the infantry of Napoleon. Closet dramas enact themselves through the night, a farce of doors opening and closing escaping psyches and entrapped satisfactions.

To someone's daughter this happens in winter while awaiting a new chance, a new year, a new number. Her mother wraps the daughter's favorite ornament in the same white tissue each year, a green glass fish, thought to dream, said to sleep.

1987
Elton Glaser, *Tropical Depressions*
Michael Pettit, *Cardinal Points*

1988
Bill Knott, *Outremer*
Mary Ruefle, *The Adamant*

1989
Conrad Hilberry, *Sorting the Smoke*
Terese Svoboda, *Laughing Africa*

1993
Tom Andrews, *The Hemophiliac's Motorcycle*
Michael Heffernan, *Love's Answer*
John Wood, *In Primary Light*

1994
James McKean, *Tree of Heaven*
Bin Ramke, *Massacre of the Innocents*
Ed Roberson, *Voices Cast Out to Talk Us In*

1990
Philip Dacey, *Night Shift at the Crucifix Factory*
Lynda Hull, *Star Ledger*

1991
Greg Pape, *Sunflower Facing the Sun*
Walter Pavlich, *Running near the End of the World*

1992
Lola Haskins, *Hunger*
Katherine Soniat, *A Shared Life*